What Is Church Government?

Basics of the Faith

Sean Michael Lucas, Series Editor

What Is Church Government?

Sean Michael Lucas

P&R
PUBLISHING
P.O. BOX 817 • PHILLIPSBURG • NEW JERSEY 08865-0817

Dedicated to my friend and colleague, David B. Calhoun, professor emeritus
of church history at Covenant Theological Seminary, who loves the church of
Jesus Christ in its Presbyterian expression throughout the world.

Page design by Tobias Design

Printed in the United States of America

Library of Congress Cataloging-in-Publication Data

Lucas, Sean Michael, 1970–
  What is church government? / Sean Michael Lucas.
      p. cm. — (Basics of the faith)
  Includes bibliographical references.
  ISBN 978-1-59638-150-6 (pbk.)
  1. Presbyterianism. 2. Church polity. I. Title.
  BX9175.3.L83 2009
  262'.05—dc22
                                      2009015322

◻**When my youngest son** was two years old, we played what we called the "name game." I would ask him, "Are you a sheepdog?" "No," he replied. "So, are you a whippoorwill?" I questioned him further. "No, Daddy," he said with a giggle. "Are you a bass fish?" I asked again with a smile. "No!" he shouted with relish. "Then who are you?" I finished. He laughed, "I'm Ben Lucas!" Even my two-year-old knew that his name conveys an identity that places him in the world.

Yet many people within and outside our Presbyterian churches fail to reckon fully with the identity the *Presbyterian* name conveys. There are beliefs, practices, and stories that shape us as Presbyterians—experiences that convey a particular approach or identity through which we encounter the world.[1] Typically we associate beliefs concerning God's sovereignty, human depravity, and Christ's particular redemption with what it means to be Presbyterian. However, those beliefs were not the main reasons our forebears were Presbyterian. Rather, Presbyterianism had its roots in a conversation about the nature and governance of the church.

The word *Presbyterian* comes from the New Testament Greek word *presbyteros*, usually translated "elder" (see Acts 11:30; 14:23; 1 Tim. 5:17, 19; Titus 1:5; 1 Peter 5:1, 5). Focusing on the New Testament usage of the word *elder* has led many to argue that the original form of church government in the apostolic church was Presbyterian—that is, oversight of local churches by elders who provided spiritual direction and discipline. However, simply pointing out the word's usage does not fully establish the case for Presbyterian church government. In fact, I suggest that the Presbyterian understanding of church government relies on as full a range of biblical and theological resources as does our understanding of the doctrines of salvation.

My hope is that this brief examination of Presbyterian church government will encourage us to commit ourselves anew to the challenge that the nineteenth-century American theologian James Henley Thornwell laid down so long ago: "We shall, therefore, endeavor to do what has never yet been adequately done—bring out the energies of our Presbyterian system of government."[2] This is all the more important because our biblical, Presbyterian understanding of church government is ultimately necessary for the preservation of those gracious doctrines that we know as the "Reformed faith." It is also necessary because this biblical teaching of what the church is and how it is to function in the world can help to meet the deep needs of our postmodern generation.

CHRIST RULES AS
THE CHURCH'S KING

In Scotland our Presbyterian forebears had a motto that summarized their understanding of the nature of the church and its relationship to the state: "for Christ's crown and covenant." The "covenant" part of that motto had to do with a national covenant signed by Scots Presbyterians who desired a unified church with England. The "crown" part of the motto expressed a profound truth on which Presbyterianism rests: Christ Jesus himself is King over his church. He has "crown rights"—his is the ultimate authority as the head and ruler over his people. No one person—whether pope or pastor or president—can usurp the place of King Jesus over his church.

I have a pastor friend who tells a story of how we can unwittingly lose sight of this truth. At a vacation bible school the teacher was leading small children in making crowns. My friend's two daughters were in this VBS class, and they dutifully made the crowns. Afterward the teacher began her lesson. "Class, what kind of person wears a crown?" The class responded, "A king! A queen!" The teacher went on, "And class, who is the King over the church?" One of my friend's daughters shouted out, "Well, my daddy is the king of the church!"

We often mistakenly believe that pastors or elders are kings of the church, the true rulers of the church. But Presbyterians have insisted on this great truth: Jesus Christ is the sole King over his church. He wears the crown, and no one else does. Historically, this confession has meant that Presbyterians have disagreed with Roman Catholics concerning the role of the pope. We've confessed that "there is no other head of the Church but the Lord Jesus Christ. Nor can the Pope of Rome, in any sense, be head thereof" (WCF 25:6).[3]

Because Jesus is King, he has all authority over his people, the church. As the Resurrected One in Matthew 28:18 he declared, "All authority in heaven and on earth has been given to me." He is the one who has all authority, all power; he is Lord over all and is seated at God's right hand (Acts 2:33; Phil. 2:7–9). The apostle Paul tells us that Jesus is head over the church, the source and ground of all authority for Christ's own body (Eph. 1:22; 4:15; Col. 1:18; 2:10).

Jesus is now executing his role as King by "calling out of the world a people to himself, and giving them officers, laws, and censures, by which he visibly governs them" (LC 45). Jesus himself governs and rules over his people today. The nineteenth-century Scots Presbyterian theologian James Bannerman put it this way:

> Within the province of the Church, the Lord Jesus Christ is the only Teacher, Lawgiver, and Judge. If doctrine is taught, it is taught because he has revealed; if ordinances are administered, they are administered in his name, and because they are his; if government is established and exercised, it is through his appointment and authority; if

saving grace is dispensed, it is dispensed through the virtue and power of his Spirit; if a blessing is communicated, it is because he blesses.[4]

Whether we recognize it or not, Jesus continues to exert his rule over his people—it is his ministry to his people for the expansion of his kingdom to the praise of his glory.[5]

HOW CHRIST RULES HIS CHURCH

The question naturally comes to us—is Jesus really ruling over his church? We sometimes look at our churches and wonder how in the world this can be. We see pastors and church members engaged in moral or financial scandals; we have experienced the pain of church ruptures; we see what appears as injustice carried on in church courts. How is it that Jesus is truly ruling over his church?

In order to get toward an answer, we need to think about the word *church* and how it is used in the Bible, especially in the New Testament. There are a couple of different ways that the Greek word *ekklesia* is used for *church*. One way might be called the "ideal" way in which the church is considered: the body of God's people through space and time who were truly elect, genuinely regenerate, and effectually united to Jesus, receiving all the benefits of his mediation. For example, when Jesus says in Matthew 16:18, "I will build my church, and the gates of hell shall not prevail against it," he means that the church as the society of the elect will not be overwhelmed by the devil, but will ultimately triumph over principalities and powers (see Eph. 6:11–12). Likewise, in Ephesians 5:25–27 when Paul says, "Christ loved the church and gave himself up for her . . . so that he might present the church to himself in splendor, without spot or wrinkle or any such thing, that she might be holy and without blemish," he means the church ideally considered, made up of the elect through the ages who are truly holy in God's sight through Christ's blood and righteousness.

Another way the church is represented is in its actual manifestation, including all those who profess the faith of Jesus throughout the world. In 1 Corinthians 1:2, Paul writes, "To the church of God that is in Corinth, to those sanctified in Christ Jesus, called to be saints together with all those who in every place call upon the name of our Lord Jesus Christ, both their Lord and ours." The divine call of the Lord is related to the individual's response, his or her calling upon the name of the Lord, a clear allusion to Joel 2:14 that Paul uses in Romans 10:13 as well as here (see also 1 Cor. 12:3). This individual calling upon the Lord's name is not localized, but extends beyond Corinth, London, New York, or Beijing; wherever the sun rises and sets, there are men and women who call upon the name of the Lord. These churches include households (Acts 16:11–15, 25–34; 1 Cor. 1:16; Eph. 6:1–3; Col. 3:20) who follow their household heads as these men and women follow Jesus. These churches often may include those who are false professors for a time or who are false teachers (1 Tim. 1:20; 2 Tim. 4:10; 2 Peter 2:1–3; 1 John 2:19).

These two ways in which the Bible speaks of the church—an ideal church and an actual church—roughly correspond to the way the Westminster Confession talks about an "invisible" and a "visible" church. Recently this way of speaking has come under increasing scrutiny within conservative Presbyterian circles. For example, John Murray, the great theologian at Westminster Seminary, once argued that

> "the church" in the New Testament never appears as an invisible entity and therefore may never be *defined* in terms of invisibility. That is why . . . the advisability of the use of the actual term "invisible" has been questioned. It is a term that is liable to be loaded with the misconceptions inherent in the concept "invisible church," and tends to support the abuses inherent thereto.[6]

While Murray and others have had laudable concerns about the way some believers use the idea of the "invisible church" for sloppiness in their approach to life in a very real and visible congregation, I think that these concerns do not warrant doing away with this way of talking about the nature of the church. In fact, I would go so far as to suggest that even if we did away with this description, we would have to develop some sort of substitute.

First, it is important that we understand how these terms are used in Presbyterian confessions. We confess that "the catholic or universal church, which is invisible, consists of the whole number of the elect, that have been, are, or shall be gathered into one, under Christ the Head thereof; and is the spouse, the body, the fullness of Him that filleth all in all" (WCF 25:1). Notice that the confession speaks of a universal church that can be viewed in its entirety only by God himself. In other words, God alone sees all those throughout time and space whom he has chosen and united to Christ by his Spirit. Neither human eye nor any visible institution can encompass all of God's elect; it is literally invisible to us.

We also confess that "the visible church, which is also catholic or universal under the gospel (not confined to one nation, as before under the law), consists of all those throughout the world that profess the true religion; and of their children" (WCF 25:2). This is the human perspective, the church that we can see—this church is also "universal" in that it is not confined to any one nation. Instead, as one historian has noted, Christianity represents the only truly "world religion," because it is spread throughout the world and has representation in virtually every nation. This church we can see in every community is made up of all those who profess Christ as well as their children. In this visible church we have "mingled many hypocrites who have nothing of Christ but the name and outward appearance" (Calvin, *Institutes*, 4.1.7) as well as those who love Jesus with all their hearts.[7]

There were very specific historical reasons why Presbyterian and Reformed believers thought about the church in these terms. The Roman Catholic Church argued that all those who were in good standing with the visible church—the Roman Church—were in good standing with God. They merged the visible church with the church that God alone can see in such a way as to identify the two. The result of a lost distinction between the church as God sees it and as we see it was a culture-religion followed by formalism, superstition, and the loss of vital biblical Christianity.

On the other side, the sixteenth-century Anabaptists (and modern-day Baptists) went to a different extreme. They believed that they could gain God's insight into who was truly regenerate and was truly part of the church as God sees it. They sought to identify this universal, "invisible" church with the visible church. Their program was to "purify" the membership of the visible church so that it matched the church that God alone can see—this, of course, was the ideal of a "regenerate church membership."

In response to the Roman Catholics and the Anabaptists, Reformers such as Calvin argued that we should have "a certain charitable judgment" toward those who "by confession of faith, by example of life, and by partaking of the sacraments, profess the same God and Christ with us" (Calvin, *Institutes*, 4.1.8). Our own assurance of others' regeneration is not necessary. They also spoke of a universal church, invisible to us, in order to make place for the reality that our knowledge of others' faith and standing with God does not match God's own knowledge.

I believe there are biblical and theological reasons for holding on to this distinction as a valid and important way to describe the church. The apostle Paul, in explaining that the promises of God to Israel did not fail, argued that "not all who are descended from Israel belong to Israel, and not all are children of Abraham because they are offspring, but 'through Isaac shall your offspring be named.' This means that it is not the children of the flesh who are the children of God, but the children of the promise are counted as offspring" (Rom. 9:6–8). Paul here suggests that not everyone who belonged to Israel *visibly*—in terms of circumcision, sacrifice, and other duties—necessarily belonged to "true" Israel: those chosen by God to be his children of promise.

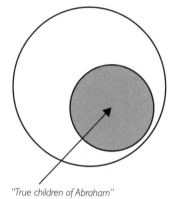

OLD TESTAMENT
Visible people of God:
All Israel (adults and children)

"True children of Abraham"

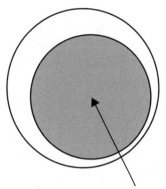

NEW TESTAMENT
Visible people of God:
Professing believers and their children

Participants in the new covenant

The diagram above illustrates "visible" Israel—all adults and children who belonged to Israel. "To them belong the adoption, the glory, the covenants, the giving of the law, the worship, and the promises" (Rom. 9:4). From the Old Testament and from what Paul says, we know that not everyone who belonged to visible Israel looked through the entire old covenant system, saw the Redeemer of God's chosen people, believed in him, and was justified by God. Therefore, within the visible Old Testament people of God, there was a remnant that represented the true children of Abraham to whom God's promises came and for whom they were fulfilled.

In the New Testament, the situation is similar. The visible people of God in Christ's church are those who have made credible professions of faith in Jesus Christ, been baptized, and participate in the Lord's Supper, along with their children. Not everyone in this number is part of the true people of God—those who truly participate in the new covenant, who receive the Spirit of God, a new heart, and all of Christ's benefits, as well as Christ himself. There are hypocrites in this number, as well as those who depart from the faith. The Westminster Confession of Faith reminds us,

"The purest churches under heaven are subject both to mixture and error" (25:5). Part of that error is represented by people who use Christ's name falsely.

By recognizing that the visible church we see does not match up to the church as God sees it, we have a workable explanation for the problem of apostasy as well as an understanding of how God's promise relates to those who identify with the visible church. As the Larger Catechism teaches us, "All that hear the gospel, and live in the visible church, are not saved; but they only who are true members of the church invisible" by God's electing grace and genuine faith in Jesus Christ (LC 61).

CHRIST DELEGATES HIS AUTHORITY

Now, it is important for us to recognize that there are not two churches, but the same church seen in two different ways—the actual ("visible church") seen by God and us and the ideal ("invisible church") seen by God alone. Christ is King over this one church. The Westminster Confession states that Christ is the head of the "invisible church" and the "visible church" is "the kingdom of the Lord Jesus Christ" (see WCF 25:1–2). Christ has authority over all those who name him, whether they are genuine or not, whether they are of age or not, whether they are able to comprehend or not. He is the King.

Christ commits his authority to his people in a variety of ways. For example, in Matthew 28 after he declares that he has all authority in heaven and earth, Jesus tells his apostles (and his later followers) to "go therefore and make disciples of all nations." This power was given to Jesus' commissioned ones to make followers of Jesus and to gather them together into the new community that Jesus was forming, based on confession of faith in him (see also Matt. 16:18–19). The means for making disciples were baptism and instruction: "baptizing them in the name of the Father and of the Son and of the Holy Spirit, teaching them to observe all that I have commanded you." And the promise attached to this authority was the continuing presence of Jesus until the end of the age (Matt. 28:16–20). Thus, Jesus' followers have power granted to them by Jesus himself to gather disciples, administer sacraments, and teach his Word authoritatively (WCF 30:1).

This authority or power delegated by Jesus is spiritual in nature. This means that the church "is a spiritual instrumentality for working out the spiritual good of man."[8] Or to put it differently, the church has a spiritual *mission*, which is nothing less than the salvation of God's people, through a spiritual *empowerment*—the very power of the Holy Spirit. Specifically, the church exercises its spiritual power in three ways.

1. The church has power to declare its doctrine. The church has authority to say that it believes certain things to be true from the Bible and other things not to be true. King Jesus has entrusted his Word to the church so that she might be "a pillar and buttress of the truth" (1 Tim. 3:15). In addition, the church's task in the post-apostolic age was to communicate the biblical witness faithfully to succeeding generations (2 Tim. 2:2), defend it from attack (Jude 3–4), present reasons for belief (1 Peter 3:15), instruct others in its truths (Matt. 28:19), and witness to its truthfulness and power (2 Peter 1:19–21).

One means that the church uses to declare its doctrine is to formulate and adopt creeds, which are summaries of biblical teaching. In the Presbyterian Church in America (PCA), our confessional standards are the Westminster Confession of Faith and the Larger and Shorter Catechisms. While written in the seventeenth century, they continue to serve as valuable summaries of biblical truths, ones that are unlikely to be surpassed in our current age. The Westminster Standards (as they are sometimes called) are valuable for their comprehensiveness, their precision, and their gospel-centeredness. Westminster Seminary founder J. Gresham Machen compared the Standards to modern-day doctrinal statements:

When we pass from these modern statements to the great creeds, what a difference we discover! Instead of wordiness we find conciseness; instead of an unwillingness to offend, clear delimitation of truth from error; instead of obscurity, clearness; instead of vagueness, the utmost definiteness and precision.

Machen suggested that these differences can be accounted for when one considers the older confession's purpose. "The modern statements are intended to show how little of the truth we can get along with and still be Christians, whereas the great creeds of the church are intended to show much of truth God has revealed to us in His Word."[9] The premise of the great confessions, such as the Westminster Standards, is that more declared truth should lead to greater unity.[10]

As doctrinal standards, they remain subordinate to Scripture. I suggest that the relationship between Scripture and confession is a hermeneutical spiral that inevitably leads to confession summarizing scriptural belief and guiding future scriptural interpretation while providing means for confessional revision. This entire spiral occurs while our confessional documents still affirm and preserve scriptural infallibility, sufficiency, and ultimate authority. Yet these doctrinal statements, while subordinate to Scripture, maintain a regulative function in the life of the church.

> The *Confession of Faith* and the *Larger* and *Shorter Catechisms* of the Westminster Assembly, together with the formularies of government, discipline, and worship are accepted by the Presbyterian Church in America as standard expositions of the teachings of Scripture in relation to both faith and practice. (BCO 29-1)[11]

It is important to have an agreed-upon standard, if for no other reason than that theological deviants have always appealed to

Scripture to sustain their views (see 1 Tim. 1:3–11). For the PCA, that standard exposition of Scripture can be found in the Westminster Confession and Catechisms.

2. The church exercises its power to order its worship and administer its sacraments. This authority to order worship is bounded by God's Word. "But the acceptable way of worshipping the true God is instituted by Himself, and so limited by His own revealed will, that He may not be worshipped according to the imaginations and devices of men, or the suggestions of Satan, under any visible representation, or any other way not prescribed in the Holy Scripture" (WCF 21:1). When the church worships, it does so according to a scriptural pattern: prayer and thanksgivings are made to the triune God; reading and preaching of Scripture (as well as "the conscionable hearing" of it); singing of biblical and biblically based prayers; and the administration of baptism and the Lord's Supper are elements of the regular and ordinary worship of God (WCF 21:2–5; see also Acts 2:42). The church does not have the authority to make up a new element of worship.

The church does have authority to order these elements, to carry out these elements in certain ways (for example, deciding whether it is appropriate or necessary to accompany singing with a tuba or a guitar or an organ; there is no biblical regulation on this), to perform or not to perform certain elements in a given service, and to schedule services on Sunday and other days as it sees fit. The church must be careful while exercising this authority not to misuse its power and unwittingly bind the people's consciences in an unbiblical or extrabiblical manner.

3. The church exercises its power by disciplining its members. We tend to think of discipline as a punitive or corrective action. However, "discipline is systematic training under the authority of God's Scripture" (BCO 27-4), which God uses to grow us in grace and to promote the "purity and welfare" of his church (BCO 27-1). Importantly, the first form of the church's discipline in a believer's life is when he or she is admitted to communicant membership. As the church's session uses the keys of the kingdom (Matt. 16:19; see also John 20:22–23 and WCF 30:2, 4) to admit professing believers to membership, this is a form of discipline. The membership process should serve to encourage and grow believers in their commitment to Christ and his church. Another type of formative discipline is pastoral counseling and care. As individuals struggle with particular types of sin or wrestle with major life decisions, work with pastors or elders on these matters, and receive advice or admonition, this serves to discipline them in the faith.

There is a more restricted form of discipline that is more corrective and formal. Even here corrective discipline is meant to build up professing believers and the church as a whole. Matthew 18:15–20 serves as a basic outline for handling discipline prior to a formal church process. If an individual sins, he or she should be confronted and admonished privately by an individual; if he or she is unwilling to hear, then two should go to admonish; and then, if he or she is still unwilling to hear the concerns, then the matter should be taken up by the church's elders in a more formal manner.

As the church's elders discipline a member, they are constantly seeking the individual's repentance. In order to draw this out, elders may find it necessary to issue a formal admonition—"the formal reproof of an offender by a church court, warning him of his guilt and danger, and exhorting him to be more circumspect and watchful in the future" (BCO 30-2). If the individual is unrepentant, it may be necessary to suspend him or her from the sacrament of the Lord's Supper. Such a suspension is always indefinite and meant to provoke the individual to examination and a change of heart and action (BCO 30-3). If that doesn't happen and if the individual is particularly unwilling to cooperate with the church (or even abandons the church altogether), the church's session may need to excommunicate the individual. Typically this action is taken only when someone has engaged in "gross crime or heresy and when the individual shows himself incorrigible and contumacious" (BCO 30-4). Even here the goal is to reclaim the sinner while protecting the reputation of the church.[12]

Sometimes we say that these three ways of exercising spiritual authority—declaring doctrine, ordering worship, and exercising discipline—are ministerial and declarative. By this we mean that the authority is rooted in the will of God revealed in Scripture. King Jesus is alone the Lord of individual consciences. His authority to bind consciences can be derived only from Holy Scripture. Even then we confess that human beings can often err in understanding the will of God found in Scripture (WCF 20:2; 31:2–3). This means that churches and their leaders must tread very carefully when exercising spiritual authority.

Because the church's power is exclusively spiritual, it is not to be confused with the power granted to the state, nor is the state to usurp the church's power. The state, with power delegated to it by God, exercises authority in temporal matters and wields coercive power on God's behalf (Rom. 13:1–7). The state has power to tax, wage war, defend its citizenry, and punish lawbreakers (WCF 23:1). The church has none of these powers, nor may it use the state's power to accomplish its spiritual mission. In fact, Jesus himself explicitly distinguished the state from the church (Matt. 22:21), differentiated between the power that civil rulers had and that which church rulers had (Matt. 20:20–28), and declared that the church's authority was a different kind altogether from that of the state because God's rule is not of this world (John 18:36–37). Because of this distinction between church and state power, Presbyterians have long confessed that the church is "to handle or conclude nothing, but that which is ecclesiastical" and is "not to intermeddle with civil affairs, which concern the commonwealth" (WCF 31:4). This commitment not to involve itself in temporal affairs recognized that the church's sphere, power, and mission is spiritual in nature and is different from the state's sphere.

CHRIST RULES THROUGH OFFICERS

As King, Jesus calls a people out of the world and gives them "officers, laws, and censures, by which he visibly governs them" (LC 45). In fact, the apostle Paul teaches us that the resurrected and ascended Christ received "gifts" to give to his church, which are "the apostles, the prophets, the evangelists, the shepherds and teachers, to equip the saints for the work of ministry, for building up the body of Christ" (Eph. 4:7–12). Through these officers (whom Christ the King gives to his church as a gift) and through his Word (which he gives as the church's law), Christ visibly governs his church.

This does not mean that only church officers have this authority, in distinction from church lay members. "The power which Christ has committed to His church vests in the whole body, the rulers and those ruled, constituting it a spiritual commonwealth. This power, as exercised by the people, extends to the choice of those officers whom He has appointed in His church" (BCO 3-1). In other words, Christ has entrusted authority to his church as a whole in order for each member to enjoy its benefits and submit to its authority. Christ has entrusted power particularly to believers within his church who are officers, so that they might administer and exercise it on behalf of the rest. As one writer put it, "[Church power] belongs equally and by Divine warrant to both; but under different characters, suited to the different places each party occupies in the Christian Church."[13]

It is important to recognize that church officers do not exercise this power on their own initiative. All church power is granted to officers through the call of Jesus Christ, which comes by the consent of the church. That is why local congregations nominate, call, and elect their own officers, both elders and deacons; no body is to be ruled by officers they do not choose for themselves (Acts 6:1–6; 14:23).

This was actually a major issue in the Church of Scotland in the nineteenth century. Thomas Chalmers, longtime pastor and professor of theology at the University of Edinburgh, argued in the courts of the church that congregations ought to have the right to issue a call to their ministers and to veto any suggested ministers that presbyteries might offer. When the Church of Scotland's General Assembly disregarded this congregational privilege to call their own officers, a large number of ministers, elders, and congregations left to form the Free Church of Scotland in 1843. This principle—that the church as a commonwealth grants authority to ministers and elders through Jesus—continues to be an important Presbyterian principle.[14]

Even when granted church power by Christ through his church, officers are not free to do whatever they wish. Power to order the church's worship is exercised by officers "severally" (or individually) only because they have been commissioned by the church for the exercise of that authority. So, for example, the authority to preach the gospel and administer the sacraments comes either through a call issued by a local church or by powers granted by a presbytery. No one takes it upon himself to preach or administer the sacraments without proper authorization.

Power of *jurisdiction* is the authority to interpret and apply the church's rules of discipline or to declare doctrinal standards. This power is exercised by officers jointly as church courts. No elder as an individual has the right to bring judgment in a discipline case; only as a group of elders, whether in a local church session, in a geographical presbytery, or in the national General Assembly of the church, can such authority be exercised. Moreover, no single elder has a right to declare doctrine that is different from what the church has already declared it believes the Bible teaches. Instead, elders who disagree with the church's confessional standards submit their views to the judgment of a session or presbytery, which decides whether to allow those exceptions to the church's doctrine (BCO 3-2; 21-4). Whether this church power is exercised individually or jointly, it has divine sanction only when it conforms to the Word of God.

Presbyterian churches have two sets of officers: one that represents oversight, and the other, service in the body of Christ. The office of oversight is called *elder*; the Greek word for *elder* (*presbyteros*) is the source of our word *presbyter*, and hence the denominational name *Presbyterian*. Elders have oversight over the church's doctrine, morals, and discipline. They "exercise government and discipline, and take oversight not only of the spiritual interests of the particular church, but also the Church generally when called thereunto" (BCO 8-3). Elders have several duties, including visiting people in their homes, caring for the sick, instructing the uninformed, comforting the mourner, nurturing the church's children, setting a spiritual example, evangelizing the unconverted, and praying with and for people.

Within this class of officers, there are two orders: "Let the elders who rule well be considered worthy of double honor, especially those who labor in preaching and teaching" (1 Tim. 5:17). This text suggests that all elders rule, but some elders also labor in preaching and teaching God's Word as a focus. *Ruling elders* are specifically entrusted with the administration of order and discipline in a particular church; in addition, they are called upon to "cultivate zealously their own aptness to teach the Bible and should improve every opportunity of doing so" (BCO 8-9). *Teaching elders* are those who, in addition to having the responsibility of ruling in the church, have the functions of feeding the flock by reading, expounding, and preaching the Word of God and administering the sacraments (BCO 8-5). Teaching elders are sometimes called *ministers of the Word*.

Both teaching elders and ruling elders have "the same authority and eligibility to office in the courts of the Church" (BCO 8-9), and both have pastoral orientation and function (BCO 8-1). In addition, teaching elders are not elders because they *teach*, but they teach because they are *elders*. That is, the right of ministers to preach within Christ's church is due to the fact that they hold the office of elder, not because they have been called as the preacher. Presbyterian churches have no special priestly class with special powers or authority; rather, the office of oversight is elder.[15]

The office of service within the church is called *deacon*. In Acts 6 the apostles, as elders of Christ's church, performed both the ministries of oversight and service. Because the task of service began to take them away from their task of oversight, they appointed those selected by God's people to serve them: "Therefore, brothers, pick out from among you seven men of good repute, full of the Spirit and of wisdom, whom we will appoint to this duty. But we will devote ourselves to prayer and to the ministry of the word" (vv. 3–4).

So from the very beginning, the office of deacon was "one of sympathy and service" (BCO 9-1). Deacons serve under the oversight of and by delegation of authority from the elders (BCO 9-2). They are spiritual men, chosen from within the body (BCO 7-2) and ordained to the office by the laying on of hands (BCO 17, 24). The deacon's responsibilities of stewardship and service include ministering to the needy, the sick, the friendless, and any in distress. Deacons also seek "to develop the grace of liberality in the members of the church," devising means for collecting the gifts of the people and for distributing the benevolences of the church (BCO 9-2). They also have oversight of the church's property, seeking to keep it maintained. It is important to notice how vital these things are for effective church ministry—only in deeds of mercy to the lost and needy will the word of God's mercy take on its fullest complexion; only in deeds of liberality and benevolence can the communion of the saints be realized; only as the church shows itself to be a good steward with material things can others trust it to be a good steward of the mysteries of God. A well-ordered diaconal ministry is vital for the church's proclamation of the gospel of God's grace.[16]

CHRIST RULES THROUGH
THE CHURCH'S COURTS

Postmoderns are bothered when Presbyterians discuss the "courts of the churches." Some suggest that this inevitably creates a litigious and oppositional approach to life together in Christ's church. However, there are good reasons to hold on to this language. The word *court* simply points to "a sovereign's governing body" or "a formal meeting or reception presided over by a sovereign."[17] The word reminds us that when elders gather together to do the work of the church, they are King Jesus' governing body, and their meetings are formal meetings presided over by King Jesus. From this perspective these courts look less like places where elders legislate and prosecute and more like formal meetings for prayer, oversight, and discipline under King Jesus' rule. They reflect God's kingdom rule expressed in Christ's current session at the Father's right hand (Acts 2:33).

The basic court of the church is the presbytery. In fact, "the Church is governed by various courts, in regular gradation, which are all, nevertheless, Presbyteries, as being composed exclusively of presbyters" (BCO 10-1). This is an important point: since all the church courts are made up of presbyters, they are all presbyteries. They are all one in nature and possess the same rights and powers, and these courts are connected in a gradated fashion. Practically, this means that matters of doctrine and discipline that are disputed in a local congregation can be referred to a regional presbytery and, from there, to a national General Assembly (BCO 11-3). These are not independent courts; rather, they bear a mutual relation to one another (BCO 11-4).

In the local congregation, the gathering of elders is called the *session*. A local church session consists of the senior pastor, associate pastor(s), and ruling elders; these have all been elected by the people to represent them under the rule of King Jesus (BCO 12-1). The session has responsibility to oversee the spiritual life and health of church members as well as the church's ministries and worship services; to examine and install ruling elders and deacons to office; and to approve big issues related to church property (BCO 12-5). It is striking that these sessional responsibilities are amazingly *spiritual*. Specifically, when sessions focus on the temporal far more than the spiritual, they have moved off-task. Sessional work is pastoral in orientation, spiritual in focus, and eternal in effects.

As already noted, local church sessions are not independent courts. Rather, they are mutually related to other church courts. The structure for these mutual relations is called the *presbytery*, which consists of "all the teaching elders and churches within its [regional] bounds that have been accepted by the presbytery" (BCO 13-1). These churches are represented at presbytery meetings by ruling elders elected by sessions. Together, these elders care for the work of the entire church in a given region. Some of a presbytery's tasks are credentialing new ministers and overseeing current ministers and licensed preachers within its bounds; planting new churches within its bounds and calling men to organize those new works; and maintaining the purity of the church, both locally and nationally, by seeking pure doctrine and advising the whole church on matters of mutual benefit (BCO 13-9). Again, the focus is on the church's spiritual mission: the extension of gospel ministry through the credentialing of gospel ministers and the defense of gospel truth.

The *General Assembly* is "the highest court of this church, [which] represents in one body all the churches thereof" (BCO 14-1). In the PCA, the General Assembly is not a "representative" assembly, strictly speaking. Every teaching elder is eligible to be a commissioner to the General Assembly (it is not representative in this regard), but the churches are represented by ruling elders in a proportional fashion (it *is* representative in this sense). This approach to representation is consistent with the principles that guide the formation of presbyteries. The practical result is that there are often twice as many teaching elders as ruling elders at the General Assembly.

Even this court of the church has a pastoral focus. It is notable that the General Assembly is supposed to serve as "the bond of union, peace, and correspondence" for the churches (BCO 14-1). In serving as such a bond, it is responsible for encouraging the membership to carry out the Great Commission. In fact, all of the agencies and committees are responsible for evaluating needs and resources—always keeping in mind the priority of the most effective fulfillment of the Great Commission.

CHRIST RULES A CONNECTIONAL CHURCH

In thinking about these church courts and how they relate to one another, we must keep in mind a very important principle. *In Presbyterianism, the parts are in the whole and the whole is in the parts.* In my opinion, this represents the heart of the Presbyterian system. There are a number of important corollaries that come from this principle. One corollary from this principle is sometimes called review and control (BCO 11-4). Each higher court has responsibility for the actions of the lower court. This is most clearly represented in the fact that the minutes and records of lower courts are reviewed by higher courts: session minutes are reviewed and approved by presbyteries; presbytery records are reviewed and approved by the General Assembly; and General Assembly minutes are reviewed by the entire church. This is also represented in the fact that presbyteries are responsible for the church's work and are charged to care for the health of all the churches in a given area. When a particular church experiences tension between the pastor and other elders, presbytery will appoint a commission to review the situation and work out a solution. This principle also plays out with the church's agencies—presbyteries appoint commissioners to General Assembly to serve on committees to review the work of the church's agencies, ensuring that the larger work is controlled by representatives of the entire body. Review and control demonstrates the mutual submission of the parts of the church to the whole and the whole to its parts (BCO 40).

This principle also means that the parts have the right of appeal to the whole. If a minority within a court believes that the majority has acted contrary to Scripture or to the order by which the church has agreed to abide, they have the right to bring the court's action to the notice of the whole church. Sometimes this is represented by a reference, sometimes by an appeal, and sometimes by a complaint. Each of these actions has specific requests made of the higher court by a minority in a lower court. A *reference* is a request by a lower court to a higher one seeking advice or other action on a matter before the lower court (BCO 41-1). When a court's action goes against a church member, he or she has the privilege of *appeal* to a higher court, which will hear and rule on the grounds of appeal (BCO 42-1). And when a court makes a decision or action that appears to a communing member to go against the Bible's teaching or against the church's constitution, that member has the right of *complaint* to that court (BCO 43-1–2). Each of these means of appeal is a means of testifying that Jesus Christ is alone Lord of the conscience, that church courts do make mistakes, and that the parts are in the whole and the whole in the parts.

A final corollary from this principle is sometimes called the "connectional" principle: each part of the church has a responsibility to the others and to the whole. Local churches give benevolence funds to support the common work of the church in missions, church planting, and theological education. If local churches don't support the work of the whole church, opting rather to go their own way in missions or Christian education or theological education, then the whole church suffers. Likewise, one local church doesn't plant a church without the authorization of the presbytery. One reason for this is to ensure that churches are planted in such a way as not to harm the ministry of another church in near proximity (BCO 5-8).

Again, the point here is that each part of the church has a responsibility to care for the whole.

Another example of our connectional nature is the fact that doctrinal error or moral lapses in one part of the church affect the entire church. In cases when a presbytery is unwilling to deal with significant doctrinal or moral deviancy, two other presbyteries might request the General Assembly to assume "original jurisdiction" of the case in order that the matter might be handled for the good of the whole church (BCO 34-1). We are not allowed simply to close our eyes to doctrinal or moral problems going on in one of our presbyteries. Rather, each part of the church has a responsibility to the church as a whole to deal with such situations appropriately.

There is a difference between a network of congregations and a connectional church. That difference comes in the principle of mutual relation expressed through practices of review and control, which are at the heart of Presbyterianism. While a network of congregations may or may not notice or care when a sister church is going astray—or they may care but remain powerless to do anything—biblical Presbyterianism . has processes in place to deal with the issues. And while some in a network of churches may view their alliance as a temporary means toward a desired end, those who believe that Presbyterianism is biblical would say that the connection, the unity, that our churches share cannot be cast aside so easily. To leave such a connection thoughtlessly or without sufficient biblical grounds would be schism. Because schism is a "formal and willful separation from the unity of the church," it must rest upon profoundly doctrinal grounds in which the very gospel itself is at stake.[18] Presbyterianism serves as a biblical polity to express in a visible fashion the unity of Christ's church.

There are some who believe that any interest in a particular branch of Christ's church is inherently sectarian and strikes at the fundamental unity and catholicity of the church. It is important to say in response that some of our best theologians affirmed

Presbyterianism while not "unchurching" Christians in other denominations.[19] Even more, I believe that Presbyterian polity (as well as its larger confessional commitments) provides resources to support an evangelical catholicity, a careful engagement with other churches out of a deep understanding of what the Bible teaches and the gospel requires. As we witness to the apostolic faith, we declare common cause with all those who love King Jesus and wait for his return.

We can affirm the one, holy, catholic, and apostolic church only as we return again and again to the Bible as God's revealed will for his people. As we do this, we find these great biblical principles that shape the way we understand the doctrine of the church—principles that teach us that the church is ruled by King Jesus, by his Word declared and applied by elders as a manifestation of his reign in this time between times. In other words, these biblical principles that teach us how Christians "ought to behave in the household of God, which is the church of the living God, a pillar and buttress of the truth" (1 Tim. 3:15), also teach us the outlines of Presbyterian church government. In holding to this pattern of God's household, far from being sectarian, we actually witness to the unity and catholicity of King Jesus' church as revealed in his Word.

Hopefully, this brief explanation of Presbyterian church government is an encouragement. Many evangelicals worship and serve in churches where it is not clear how decisions are made or who is actually in charge. Sadly, some believers have even experienced the pain of abusive churches where a pastor or other church leader misused spiritual authority. What we Presbyterians confess is that King Jesus is in charge over his church: that we live, worship, and serve for Christ's crown and covenant in such a way that we will be a people "faithful to the Scriptures, true to the Reformed faith, and obedient to the Great Commission." Our great hope and expectation is that through his church, Christ is uniting all things in himself, things in heaven and things on earth, for his glory (Eph. 1:10). May God make it so!

NOTES

1 See Sean Michael Lucas, *On Being Presbyterian: Our Beliefs, Practices, and Stories* (Phillipsburg, NJ: P&R, 2006). This booklet is an expanded and revised version of sections from chapters 4 and 8.

2 James Henley Thornwell, "Address to all Churches of Christ," in *The Collected Writings of James Henley Thornwell*, ed. John B. Adger and John L. Girardeau, 4 vols. (Richmond: Presbyterian Commitee of Publication, 1873), 4:463.

3 *WCF* is an abbreviation for *Westminster Confession of Faith*, which, along with the Westminster Larger Catechism (LC) and Shorter Catechism (SC), serves as the doctrinal standard of the Presbyterian Church in America (PCA). The Westminster Confession of Faith is available online at http://www.pcanet.org/general/cof_preface.htm.

4 James Bannerman, *The Church of Christ*, 2 vols. (Carlisle, PA: Banner of Truth, 1974), 1:195.

5 A powerful presentation of this understanding can be found in the first point of the preface "The King and Head of the Church," in *The Book of Church Order of the Presbyterian Church in America*, 6th ed. (Lawrenceville, GA: Office of the Stated Clerk of the PCA, 2006).

6 John Murray, "The Church: Its Definition in Terms of 'Visible' and 'Invisible' Invalid," in *Collected Writings of John Murray*, 4 vols. (Carlisle, PA: Banner of Truth, 1976), 1:234–35.

7 John Calvin, *The Institutes of the Christian Religion*, ed. J. T. McNeill, trans. F. L. Battles, 2 vols. (Philadelphia: Westminster, 1960). All references in the text are to this edition.

8 Bannerman, *Church of Christ*, 1:24.

9 J. Gresham Machen, "The Creeds and Doctrinal Advance," in *God Transcendent*, ed. Ned B. Stonehouse (Grand Rapids: Eerdmans, 1949), 149.

10 James Bannerman put it this way: "What is the principle of union in any Christian Church which holds the truth of God as the very foundation on which it exists? Plainly and undeniably the mutual and common understanding as to the doctrine of God's Word of those associated together to constitute the Church—their union together in one common profession of the truth" (Bannerman, *Church of Christ*, 1:296).

11 *BCO* refers to the *Book of Church Order of the Presbyterian Church in America*, 6th ed. (Lawrenceville, GA: Office of the State Clerk of the PCA,

2006). All references to *BCO* in the text are to this edition, available online at http://www.pcanet.org/BCO/.

12 *Incorrigible* describes someone who is "not corrigible; bad beyond correction or reform" (http://dictionary.reference.com/browse/incorrigible). *Contumacious* is an adjective that describes someone who is "stubbornly perverse or rebellious; willfully and obstinately disobedient" (http://dictionary.reference.com/browse/contumacious).

13 Bannerman, *Church of Christ*, 1:271.

14 For more on the Disruption of 1843, see Stewart J. Brown, *Thomas Chalmers and the Godly Commonwealth in Scotland* (New York: Oxford University Press, 1982).

15 For more on this, see classic statements by Robert J. Breckinridge: "Presbyterian Government Not a Hierarchy, but a Commonwealth," *Southern Presbyterian Review* 33 (1882): 258–90, and "Presbyterian Ordination Not a Charm, but an Act of Government," *Southern Presbyterian Review* 33 (1882):463–518. These are available online at http://www.pcahistory.org/HCLibrary/period icals/spr/v33/33-2-3.pdf and http://www.pcahistory.org/HC Library/periodicals/spr/v33/33-3-2.pdf.

16 For more on diaconal ministry, see Timothy J. Keller, *Ministries of Mercy: The Call of the Jericho Road* (Phillipsburg, NJ: P&R, 1997) and Timothy J. Keller, *Resources for Deacons: Love Expressed through Mercy Ministries* (Lawrenceville, GA: Christian Education and Publications, 1985).

17 http://dictionary.reference/browse/court

18 F. L. Cross and E. A. Livingstone, *The Oxford Dictionary of the Christian Church*, 3rd rev. ed. (New York: Oxford University Press, 2005), s.v. "schism." See also Calvin, *Institutes*, 4.1.10–16.

19 For example, the nineteenth-century Presbyterian theologian James Henley Thornwell proclaimed that "we are not ashamed to confess that we are intensely Presbyterian. We embrace all other denominations in the arms of Christian fellowship and love, but our own scheme of government we humbly believe to be according to the pattern shown in the Mount, and, by God's grace, we propose to put its efficiency to the test" (Thornwell, "Address to all Churches of Jesus Christ," in *The Collected Writings of James Henley Thornwell*, 4:463). See also his "Church Boards and Presbyterianism," in ibid. 4:293–94.